A FRIENDSHIP WITH TIME

A FRIENDSHIP WITH TIME

Bibhu Padhi

HORNBILL PRESS

A FRIENDSHIP WITH TIME
A collection of Poems by Bibhu Padhi
ISBN: 978-93-87885-80-6
Cover Photo © Buddhaditya Padhi
First Published in 2021 by
Hornbill Press
Price: Price: ₹249 / $11.99 / €9.99

A Unit of Atmajaa Media Ventures Pvt. Ltd.
2/6, B. L. Ghosh Road, Kolkata – 700057
Phone: +91-9432718042, +91-6289457589
E-mail: presshornbill@gmail.com; info@hornbillpress.co.in
Website: www.hornbillpress.co.in
Copyright © 2021 Bibhu Padhi

Typeset in Garamond by Atmajaa Digital
Printed in India at Sharat Impressions Pvt. Ltd.

For

Usha, Mariam, Anjana

Acknowledgements

I am grateful to the editors of the following magazines, in which some of these poems were first published:

The Rialto, Rosebud, Oyez Review, The London Magazine, The Manhattan Review, Studio One, New Reader Magazine, New English Review. Plainsongs, North Dakota Quarterly, Willow Review, Straylight, The Awakenings Review, Pudding Magazine, I-70 Review, California Quarterly and *The Wallace Stevens Journal.*

How strange to know yourself as alive!

Octavio Paz

Contents

MID-JULY RAINS

It's night and they are falling again.
Rebirth seems to take hold of us.
Old desires fall, drop by drop, are
gathered on cupped palms like nearer things.

The wet earth echoes the sound
of the sky. I am enclosed by
the superstitious safety of my home
and wish I were out in the rains.

I know how badly I need them, how
I need to feel what heaven is, see
how blessings fall and accumulate
at our backyards, like shining pools of

fresh, infant water, though rarely noticed
by anyone at all. It certainly
would have been otherwise, but
I'm so far away from childhood now.

ALONE

What grows on life, except faith
and hope, what leaves sustain our trust
in our very own love for life's variety?

An innocent, human curiosity
that lays its foundation on belief,
a simple give and take, an old love?

How else does one frame a question
so it might not fetch a blunt, savage
answer, an unseasonal shedding of leaves?

The day has shed the leaves of a whole
lifetime's effort to be good to the world,
bring it as much happiness as one can give.

How else does one live so one might not be
thought to be blind, insane, or just not right?
A long, unrelieved burden on the world and me?

HARVESTING

The first day of a whole year's harvest
is blissfully here, in need of your
prayers, submission to heaven.

The world eagerly waits for your
devotion and effort, your
green finger's care.

Isn't there something glorious
in all that we do? There is something
fecund and good in the hot
Baisakhi atmosphere.

Something that must be taken
notice of, notwithstanding
our separate griefs, dispensable prides.

The very seeds of our lives
are here, to be sown away into
an all-accepting earth's ancient, subsoil air.

DISAPPEARANCES
For Sufia

They have been here, with me,
quite often, ever since mother left us.
That was the first time I noticed
the absence of trees and then,
a couple of years later, all the greens.
And then today, there is something I can't
quite remember, but know it was
here all the time. I recall how,
talking about it to my wife
and my little girl who never forgets
things she has once heard about
or touched. What do I tell her,
what to my wife, who has by now
got used to numerous disappearances
of things that I thought belonged to me?
Houses, addresses, poems, letters?
How do I explain these to myself?
Were they indeed mine or
someone else's, given only for my
safekeeping, under lock and key?
But do the greens care
for my stupid, inefficient fingers?
I have this feeling; these will go on forever.

A WAY TO PRAY
ON AN APRIL MORNING

Stay where you are. You will
hear the almost-zero sound
that stays on with you.

Not the sound
of the old bus gurgling
out its own smoke;

not the sound
of mosquitoes crackling
against a killer-net.

Nor the illegible sound
of your own breath
through the body's chemistry.

No. Another sound
accompanying you wherever
you go, turning with your turns,

enveloping you as if
in a circle, expanding, including
all that you are, you are not—

your dreams, illogical
thoughts, the rumors
that always travel with you,

your days and nights,
ever-shifting thoughts.
Like Creation,

a discovery. Stay in it;
watch your thoughts.
and then close your

eyes and see how empty
the mind is, as if
it was not there at all.

LOCAL DETAILS

1.

The lean, bare tree
goes by, and here is

one more just receiving
its first greens of the year.

And there is a *krishnachuda*—
intoxicated with colours.

National Highway 42 continues
through the greens,

and turns of deodars that stay
the same throughout the year.

Early summer in Dhenkanal,
and the mango trees are

blossoming to their fruits.
But just a little after, a rush

of colours. No-greens, but a flourish
of crimson-red, blinding yellow;

and no waiting for end or
beginning, as if all were here.

- Bibhu Padhi -

In the distance, on
both sides of the road,

layers of mountain-blue
kissing Creation.

2.

The details fade; they always
do. Are indistinct, then absent.

What does one
begin with then, carry

the lines without
putting off the sensitive minds?

Night is coming
to its end earlier than
it did a month ago;

summer has taken away
an hour or two from its
full, calculated length.

As I sit on my bed,
having been aroused

from a much-awaited rest
while the town is still asleep,

this pen likes to tend
towards other matters

than what is only
in the mind.

Matters nearer to the heart—
darkly visible, each

as much alone
as all the others.

What is early world,
early time?

A half-hour and a room
with a bed, left alone

to themselves and these,
my fingers?

A half-hour
of all the small wishes,
now quietly remembered?

Wishes of the heart—
night-like, blurred—
while the mind is numb
with its old desires?

There is just one
open window, and the eyes
may not see further.

Thin, weightless voices
of early birds drift in
and out of this room.

- Bibhu Padhi -

A distant sound
that cannot be cured
rolls around my ears—

a sound that hardly
belongs to this world,
and tells me I am
almost at my place.

All needs seem to
end now and here,

and I wonder if the birds
the trees, other local details,
and the slowly clearing air
hear it to.

.

MATTERS OF THE HEART

What has happened to you,
primeval lover, so that nothing—
no words of consolation

or advice—can keep you
quiet and steady, at your old,
appointed place?

As if you were delaying
an old illness that refuses
to respond to every kind

of earthly remedy, every effort
toward what now is already
a much-wished for

cure? What magical,
angelic touch can heal
your hurt? Ancient lover,

what mode of sacrifice
will work like magic, can
once again bring you near?

- Bibhu Padhi -

AFTER A LONG PAIN
For Sudeep

After a long pain, a touch alone stays—
alien, far from all you have known
from books and pictures, scientists'
discoveries, wisdom's speeches.

The mind finally feels distant, the body
is drawn away from its basic functions, feels
too amply satisfied to remember itself
or other bodies, other worlds.

Body and mind are entwined in compassion
for the heart's much-dislocated spaces
and years, hopes and tears that could
never be what they were meant to be,

while the passive earth looks on and withdraws
into itself, as if it was thinking of something
gone wrong somewhere in the universe—
something it had never witnessed or understood.

It is late morning, and there are invitations
from faraway places, each to be attended to,
taken notice of, each to be believed
as something where no pain could ever be, no tears.

Every small thing is busy recollecting itself
in the very middle of a whirlpool of disbelief, even as
the same feeling quietly relaxes, recalls each pain and
insult, each piece of advice, each earlier body.

CHOICES

When it comes to choosing
from more than one pain,
tears emerge from secret places;
the belief in oneself is eroded
by the smallest differences.
They all seem to come from
the same place, carrying similar
lonelinesses. The mind and the heart
suffer attacks of an elaborate grief
that is beyond all choosing,
all available rules of choice
and exclusion. The tears
come forth again, against
your wish, even as you feel
weak and alone, while the world
moves on its old road
of forgetting all that is close
to you, including those
much-diffused tears of a while ago.
Alien eyes suspect the story behind
your residual tears, even as you
turn away, remember—
more than ever before—your
own stories of loss, how
you were excluded in story
after story by someone else's
grief over choices
and the consequent pain of loss.

- Bibhu Padhi -

WHERE ARE THE WORDS?
For Sharmila

The darker meanings are
still there, asking us
to shut our eyes
to their shadows.
My mind and skin are loved
by thin figures, absences.

Invisible signals tell me
of new arrivals on the body's
sensitive horizons, the mind's
peripheral receptors.
There is hardly anything
to learn, any magnetic story

to be narrated passionately
before a stunned listener.
Every earlier need
has been taken care of
by vast distances, solitude,

a needlessness for words
that now dance on
other lips at different places,
under a blinding sun.
And, it is at these hours
that I wait for you, your

distant-seeming eyes,
a slight kiss on
what appears to be
a pair of muted lips,
a long-gone world for
lack of love and care.

NIGHT'S NECESSITY

Darkness descends
on churches,
mosques and temples,

on each place and object
too large for
this frail, frail faith.

I look inside
what indeed is
a house of hearts.

A dark luminosity
flashes over floors,
walls, ceilings.

There is no need
of night here,
which now is where

temples, mosques
and churches lie like some
old breath of a frayed time.

ENCLOSED

I have been exposed to
a lie-like love, a mere show
of new life and darkness.

Here my world is
born again, undisclosed
to the envious eye.

Now, in your love's
rain-shadow,
I am enclosed.

VOICES FROM THE SKY

Who keeps reminding me,
"This is not the place for you"?
Who says, "You should look
elsewhere for what you wish,
what you so badly need?"

Yes, I know I've been here
for a long while, in the flames
of controversies and hushed talk,
burning all the time; I've been
feeling weary and weak.

The days and nights move
around me like pictures on a screen—
moments of a passionate reciprocity
between the heart and the mind,
body and body, thrown open
to the violence of time.

Who says, "This place
doesn't believe in love and peace"?
Who says, "Leave, else you'll suffer
the burden of unopened hearts,
the storm of evil minds,
the language of faithlessness?"

I confess I haven't yet learnt to be
happy with myself, have forgotten
to behave in the usual ways. And all that was
given to me during an earlier century
as gifts, have been lost on the way

to this place, lost utterly. But I
know too that I needed to be here
to break my ancient promises
to a world that never cared for

what I was ready to give. Now,
I am alone, all alone with myself
and a loss that I must carry forward
to a place without love or faith—
a place that would have lost
the memory of things.

LISTENING

What is it that surrounds me?
A feeling that hardly touches me,
yet holds me as I float around,
like someone in love for the first time,
feeling himself always accompanied by
someone else? A feeling of listening to
a voice that always speaks without
making a sound? Following me
like a familiar spirit that envelops
more than just the body, seeping
into every cell, yet not staying on
for an understanding? Just here,
without a purpose, hanging in the air,
yet joined to nothing else?
Simply, invisibly building up
the feeling of the universe?
A sense of sound diffusing into
the soul's farthest places?
Bringing in the universe to the same spot
that I am at, was, will always be
in the absence of this body?
But what has it got to do with me,
when the world turns away, thinking of
the always and the insanity of speech
of each moment? What is this strange
inclusion of all space, all time?
What non-insistence surrounds
this meaningless being, keeps it
ever awake night and day?
Which unknown presence
accompanies me to wherever

- Bibhu Padhi -

I move each and every minute,
without fail, as if I were its
only friend or lover?
Until everything is separated
from its source, floats in a
landscape of doubt and disbelief?

MISSING HISTORY
For Phil Fried

By the time you know, everything
is hidden in time's wandering eye.
Places and persons unvisited for lack of time,

now borrowed from a lost mouth
for the first time. The waiting is all there is,
to be measured by an inappropriate loss—

a question to time. Suffering and loss
place you in possession of small things,
long forgotten and now remembered.

An evening's conversation offering
a missing link—a tremble on the lips, a story
untold for lack of a listener.

And then, all at once everything falls
into place—a recognition of a lost word
or face, a return to the calendar years,

and a feeling of trust in this moment's
announcement, its truth of things, emerging
now at a blurred distance of insanity.

- Bibhu Padhi -

AFTERNOON IN SUMMER, CUTTACK

Sleep thickens, spreads to include
all that you love to possess.
There are layers of invisible meetings
and conferences somewhere
between one lucidity and another.
Stories of butterfly
gather and disperse. Someone is
listening to everything, so
don't ask further questions
about your children, the past
or the world. There is always
someone to smile without an answer—
someone who has been deferring
his leaving to be a witness
to your meetings, call for meetings,
someone who quietly gets up on an
afternoon like this, to announce
"All that is visible is not of any use."
The rest follows in ragged lines
of black and white. Afternoon.
Inside the air-conditioned coach,
except your companion and yourself,
everyone is asleep and dreaming.

SUMMER ADDRESSES

They keep arriving, defying
the summer heat, the crowding
of old thoughts in the mind's

secret corners, defying
the mood to celebrate
the presence of old

relationships now, at this
moment's looking back
at all those things we lost

in our journey toward
ourselves, in a mood's revival
through a slight, healing touch.

The addresses keep rushing in,
and we wonder if they are necessary
in the mistaken adventures of the bodies.

- Bibhu Padhi -

HISTORY

It is always what you never wanted it to be—
a pair of eyes looking for the precise spot
where some of us stood harmlessly, but only
in the vicinity of death, without ever knowing

that the one way everything has worked finally
is a long story of resurrections and defeats,
and a magically inevitable life, and yet hanging loose
on the hooks of time, of faith and disbelief.

You wonder how else the burden of life
is eased, made less heavy, except through dying.
There might be other answers beyond what you think
to be true, but I know you are at the end of it all.

There is blood all over your home, where you
used to sit for a quiet hour of tea or coffee, where,
under a full-moon-sky, you sang your children to sleep,
where you wished your wishes, crafted your dreams.

I seem to guess what you think of the future,
though it may not be when or where you think it might
be, how. You should know better, having known
about it all in your so many different guises through history.

Whatever else it is; it is always different from
what you or I thought to be. Hopeless,
and a little too noisy for a heart that has consoled
itself long enough in matters that don't really belong to it.

THIS ADDRESS

These days, to put it down
is a quick pain in the fingers,
a sharp flame somewhere
in the mind, the loss of a heartbeat
in the very middle of the usual hour.

I wonder if it is right
to continue with the old,
the nearly forgotten, but now
abused by causes that are
beyond my power to dislodge.

I suppose it should keep changing
with our many departures
and new arrivals;
it seems it should be where
we are now, at this morning hour.

I have thought of changing it, but
the heart feels disappointed, its
simple voice quietly disappearing
into itself, its quarters haunted
by ghosts of another time.

So I am bound to the strange old
address, by an instinct that is
difficult to get over, despite all change,
each shift of territory, every mode
of dispossession and human anger.

ANOTHER NEED

You have spent your years
asking for nothing, and when
someone tells you, you will

never get anything without
asking for it, you have said,
that is not my business;

the days and nights should know;
the single universal force
must respond to my needs

as it always does
to everything else, including
the earth's quiet rotation

round the sun, or a sapling's
slow rise through space and time.
But I say, they had asked for it

time and again; asking is giving,
no more, no less. I will not ask for
things, you say. You say, I am rich

already with things I never asked for.
You may not know, but silences
have their own modes of prayer

just as words have, but different,
less visible, perhaps less conceited too.
I cannot ask for things even in

silence, for words left me one night
long ago, without my asking for it.
Perhaps, that night you dreamt of it?

BODY

This is where everything
is, lives and breathes
or just ceases to be.
Everything else—all that
promises to be true—is vague
and nameless, like someone
you have never spent time with.

This alone is branches and leaves,
fingers, toes and lips, the fruit's
and the breast's haughty,
self-contained accuracy,
the statue's slow,
incredible formation through
time, each moment's limitlessness.

How can I forget what has grown
through a careful, evolving
history, or can bring in tomorrow
long before its chosen time?
Spirit of it all, it has its needs too—
the dark smell of the cave's depth,
the very special intimacies.

A QUESTION OF FAITH

Someone who cares for me, says,
"You have been so different during
these past few days. Your smiles
haven't been like your usual smiles,
your words not like your habitual words."

The mind seems to have
turned the other way—
the way the wind comes from,
the way the trees look toward to find
where all other good things are, how

they are being treated by people
who so cleverly think they belong
to the world the most proper way,
how carefully they build themselves.

My reply is a question too: "A tired
smile? Do you think so? Something
for which I appear to be putting in
a lot of effort even while this frail body
wouldn't permit me to do so?"

"Right," she says, "but we really need
the love which is so much like you.
Uncontaminated, like the upper air,
the ever-renewing wish of the short grass
for heaven, not a cold, distant smile."

I've nothing much to say, but it seems as if
I am taking something away from myself,

losing my knowledge of things their quick
successions, my faith, even my faith in
what I should indeed be for others' sake.

EARLY

October. It is rather early
even by date and desires.
And there is
a lonely winter's
fugitive touch
on the skin, in the air.

It is too early to predict
any new arrival, but
the earlier-than-usual sunsets
have been too quiet,
too invisible for the mind
for over a week now.

The provincial town
sleeps into late afternoon.
And when it is dark,
the lights appear too tired
to offer a whole day's
affection or desires.

- Bibhu Padhi -

THE OLDER TOUCHES

There are times when I remember
all of them fondly enough for them
to be here once more, all around
this house, which is far away from
where they were, and, at this hour,
far away again from my childhood fears.

Now I can just think of them. And
what is thinking except the mind's
imaginings, the heart speaking to itself
in the darkness, fearing alien
ears, the world's participation
in our daily activities?

It was a long time back. My father who
died young, enclosed me
with his feeble hands and sang his
usual song of orphaned eyes,
tears showing themselves
for the first time.

It seems I need it now. The warmth
of an ancestral touch now withered away
into history. No one knows. No one
cares to know. Except my mother, now
floating somewhere in the skiy of
yesterdays. I used to receive her touches too.

And grandmother's. Precious, like nothing else.
Her hands pressing my tired limbs with love,
fingers moving happily through my hair

in a familiar act of ritual, as if without it
her own life would have remained
incomplete, a mere leaning toward the end.

Other touches have followed. In dreams
or when I am alone and afraid of the ways
of the world. But reluctant, as if their giving
were a kind of losing, as if they meant nothing
in a world that had learnt to live with itself. And,
that is indeed when I need them most.

- Bibhu Padhi -

ANOTHER ERRATIC DAY

Even the hour of the gods
is too early for you.

You need to return to
your drug-induced sleep,
take a couple of hours more
for the night's completion.

The day is consumed by
an isolation that the gods alone
should know, a defeat of sorts
that you may not accept.

Follow the route of silence,
someone seems to say.
That is where everything
is simplified.

You know, the hour of the gods
stretches through the day;
there is always a way
to give your heart away.

But I am not the one to tell you
how, for I too long for sleep for now.

SOMETHING KEEPS HAPPENING

Something keeps happening
all the time, even in sleep,
here, in the milk-white distance
of a slow moon's fecund light.

Fluid figures move freely
in small and large spaces,
framed in by their own loss,
their wish to be noticed.

But there are times when everything
is shut and closed. Coloured circles
and spots of blue and morning-red
are engaged in a glorious dance.

You ask yourself, is it for this
I have lived all these years?
Is it for this I've been trying
to locate myself in the world?
These nameless, numberless figures?

All the while the heart has been
listening to itself. It whispers,
"No, you are too innocent to see
the hidden lie. You are not this."

And then you look the other way—
deeper, farther—as far as your mind can go.
There is this absence, this vacancy that
quietly shows, the silence that refuses
to define itself, the lightness of it all.

- Bibhu Padhi -

A FALLING IN LOVE

For a long time I haven't loved myself,
this body and all that it calls mine,
all that has risen in time.

I have only struggled to come to terms
with all that belongs to another place,
all that was never mine.

Years have passed in the darkness
of a world that had lost itself
among words and incoherence.

There have been lovers in plenty—
girls who knew well how to
use things and cleverness.

There have been too many thoughts
to comply with, or none at all;
the bed I sleep in knows how.

But today, at this quiet hour of intimacy,
I realize how beautiful the body can be,
how real the eyes, what it does not find:

the soul's prayer to be ever with it,
the mind's easy games, a secret wind's
loving pressure on the skin.

There are other affections too, other wishes
that generate energy and life, far from
neuralgia, migraine and a reasonless lethargy.

- A Friendship With Time -

I guess, this body is fine as it is and I need not
ask for more than it needs, more than
just life's happy residency.

Let money grow on trees, the rich prosper
enough to turn into gods, but please, let me
stay here, with this body, this generous time.

- Bibhu Padhi -

MIDNIGHT DISAPPEARANCES

You said you were feeling better,
much better than you had ever
in your forty-eight-year life. You smiled
at your husband and children
and it seemed you were returning
to this, our world, after a long time.
But did you know about the snow
in your chest that wouldn't melt,
had in fact quietly drained your
native warmth over the years
of an inhuman self-neglect?
Do you remember what happened
after you had said what you said?
How can you remember, for
you were slowly becoming
a part of midnight and darkness,
a disappearance that never shows itself?
You are gone, and today, three nights later,
I remember you, your slow walk toward
your classroom, your speechless profile
in the staff room, absorbed in a past
that never existed, a future
that was never meant to come.
I remember that afternoon when I
sat beside you and asked you to teach me
how to be quiet like you. You half jumped
off your chair and then smiled, as if I had
asked for a little too much;
the humility of being embarrassed
could be yours only.
Today I remember you and ask

myself, why did you have to go
when proud people pride themselves
over their stupid achievements?
I remember you, secretly, for I think
I've learnt from you what life could be,
what it certainly is not.
Bless us from where you are, forgive
this world for all its ignorance and mistakes.
Be happy with yourself.

- Bibhu Padhi -

TRYING TO FIND THINGS

It seems during all these years
I have been waiting for things
to arrive on their own—
a phrase, a line, an event
that tells its own story.
I have refused to realize
how strenuous it can be,
how far from where truth is.
It seems one must look for
things, locate the right place,
become a part of the magic
of the world, turn to a secret
that always changes its name
and shape, moves beyond itself
every second of a solitary time.
It has been rather late in knowing
this, following a voice that can be
hardly heard among the world's
noises and elaborate rituals
in which one may not believe.
Today is another day—
it was never there in the past—
and so gives one a chance
to change, become one with
all things, including those
that are so very much absent.

A NIGHT OF BLESSINGS

Before its arrival, there are messages
that announce its arrival, in words
and images, each much like the others.

As if you had forgotten its arrival
among the past years and time's
daily demands, routine consequences.

Now it is not far from where you are,
among your children and their mother,
your needless wishes, your fear of the future.

You are freshly awake from your late
afternoon sleep, that usually makes you
forget the day's earlier pressures.

You begin to remember, recall each
dark departure while your senses were alert
through your lifetime's strenuous layers

of additions and deletions, multiplications of
what you were told, were merely trials of strength;
divisions of happiness, joy and cheer.

You slowly turn toward the gathering dark,
the night of promises. You wait for your
forthcoming prayer, each word, line and pause,

the way you must look into the night, your
hands holding the candle's light, your eyes
searching for the stars you can recognize

as your own, for each is now an absence,
a long-forgotten withdrawal from where
you are, each watching you and all that is yours,

each waiting to be watched through the night,
with love and care, so it might shower on you
its loving care, plentifully, for the rest of the year.

The night would last for one night only
and you ought to remember that too
and also the irregularities of the future.

The vicious angles to this wonderful world and life,
the abrupt ends, the unnecessary extensions while
too many good things around you are falling to a close.

All around you there are sounds of crackers
to keep the night awake, lights to show
the way to your home, your wounds and fears.

They would be here anytime now, with their
invisible fingers of cure and consolation, their
blessings and infinite love, their smile of contentment.

Wait, see how somewhere there a star leaves
its allotted place to rush down to be as near you
as you need it to, fold you in, in its quiet divinity,

its hands of watchfulness and love. After all,
it all comes only once in a year and there is nothing
that wants to lose its chance to be near what it

loves and needs to be with, even if it is for a night.
For another chance, it has to wait for another year—
just like you and all those who are in need of love and care.

AGAIN, LOVE

The taste of last evening's sadness
is still in the mouth.

A sadness of love, its absences,
the world's reluctance
to take notice of it.

All those who I thought were mine,
are busy finding their own
explanations, fluent like

their own past, as if they knew
all that was going to happen.

As it was yesterday, I am all heart,
inarticulate in its efforts

to say something that might matter
at some point in the distant future.

As always, love is elsewhere, at some
gloomy station of this vastness

that is supposed to be my lot,
waiting to be noticed, taken care of.

And I am so far away, so much lost
to myself, I don't even know
where it waits.

Perhaps I should soon be leaving
this place, which I call mine.
I have a reason. Love is quietly dying.

- Bibhu Padhi -

ANNIVERSARY
for Buddhaditya and Siladitya

Somewhere a whole year hides
among our daily wishes and fears.

We don't know how years and days
are made to return on any one day.

They have their own ways of returning
to a pair of hands, a love, a place.

They do, and we suddenly discover
how far away we are from where we were

or wanted to be a year ago, on this day, for
so many things have changed, except the date.

The world hasn't changed much though
since we began, nor will, being

what it has been through time—
a mere collection of facts and necessities.

Love smiles, is silent, like memory.
Touch is on the bodies, but in the old ways.

But prayers, dreams and blessings still seem
to float low in the early December sky,

despite all our dark, collective ignorance.
As if it needed to stay, all through

another year. Let it stay.

THIS DISEMBODIED VISITOR
for Siladitya

A nameless something keeps returning
to a tender throat, periodically, despite
all our concerned efforts to keep it off
the lean innocence and helplessness
of the sinless but inflamed voice,
the body's cryptic heat, our fears.
Why does it choose to be so? As if
it would feel lonely without being
where it was, as if it was slowly making
this throat its home, safe from the world's
curious eye, as if it was its last shelter?
Our guesses move from word to word,
very human help to help, while the throat
darkly awaits the visitor's arrival
after a period of its inexplicable absence,
its possible flight to other, unsuspecting,
but less habitable throats. We wonder about
the much-required end, about how to
stop its next arrival before it has arrived.
We go through our rich vocabularies,
tell each other, "No, now that we have
chosen a very different word of warning—
the most illegible, the least administered,
almost a *mantra*—it wouldn't dare
arrive again, for it would hear and feel it
for the first time from so near."
We wait. The first sensation of its coming
is in the mind and in the air. My hopes
stay close to me though, as if they were

prayers too. I ask my child, "How do you feel
this morning, now?" A timid voice answers,
"I don't know." And I think I tell him,
"You've nothing to fear now, and this
you should know." The insistent visitor
is nowhere near, but I can still see how,
on my child's eyes,
the fear is going to stay.

MY OCTOBER LOVER

You had opened my packet of gifts.
Your blind voice over the phone
said, "I found only a diamond,
a pearl, and a drop of tear."

A shock, and the thought that
I had lost the tears a long ago,
among precious stars on a moonless
sky, hallucinations of past lives.

I don't know what I was to you
when you so kindly visited me
and chose to sit at my feet, on the cold
bare floor. "I'm a monk," you said.

I asked for your hand, my fingers
traveling over your palm, pressing your
diamonded fingers, feeling their sadness
of breath. You asked, "What is in a hand?"

You didn't know, but I was seeing
in you someone who had been
too near yet too far from me
over the barren years.

I don't know what took place
after that, what I did or did not,
till I found my lips kissing, my mouth
holding, your pearl-like toes, your tears.

I can't say if you found the Buddha
in me, but I had found my mother
in you—my lover over centuries
of hide and seek, gain and loss.

- Bibhu Padhi -

LUNCH TIME, DECEMBER

It is past lunch time and
everyone is at the table
except this laziness.

The day is too quiet
for anything except
a slow afternoon sleep.

The sky is too funereal
for speech. It allows only
numberless cups of steaming tea.

The earth seems to wait
for something new,
something like a revelation.

Who needs food now?
Even the food from heaven?
I suppose, there are

too many looking for food
than there is on the table—
so many, I shouldn't be here.

I am too weak
to write about it all.

BUTTERFLIES AT NOON

It is winter in Dhenkanal.
But today, the sun has turned
frank and clear. Its light
and warmth recall a loving day
in early summer.

The butterflies fly around
the magnolias. Gold-yellow,
vermilion, a brownish red,
light as air.

A self-denying freedom
follows their short, slight flights
without a noticeable touch.
Just about when your wish
settles on a leaf, a small brush
of pale yellow glides over it.

What are they after? Here, there,
further away. These plants and flowers,
that tangle of soft creepers.
What need or wish supports
their elaborate play?

You are not the one who would
possess them though.
You may not take their picture:
That is what possession is.

And just about when you try to
remember at least one, it moves up
above the colours, the lintel,

above the next floor, disappears.
Others have left already before
your eye could catch them.
Now there is only the pain with which
you are so familiar. And a sun that is
so near, you wish you were not here.

LIVING ON THE MARGINS

I keep counting the grains
every day, just to see how many
go into my children and wife's
lunch or dinner. There are also times
when I persuade others to do the counting
for me, for I lose my count each time
I begin—a loss that is as much mine
as of all those who have too many
grains to count them to their end.

I know, there are others who do not
count their grains, do not have to.
They just count all that they have,
just to see what was missing and hence,
must be added to fill in the spaces
they call their own, their
signature of ownership engraved on
walls and time, automobiles and speed,
private jets and priceless comfort.

I stand here, in the midst of the season of
harvesting, as much alone as when I came
to this place for the first time, without napkins
or names, without a grain in my mouth. Perhaps
that was why I wept for the first time. Now, I stand
here, alone, and see lean figures move sluggishly
at those places beyond which the eyes can't go.
I struggle to see. There are only blurred images
of a loneliness that I haven't so far known.

- Bibhu Padhi -

I think I can faintly recall a time
when I too was lonely and too fragile
to think of counting my grains at all. That
must have indeed been a long time ago, but
now, at this hour, I can slowly recall how it feels
to count one's grains and those of one's dear ones
and then suddenly find there was in fact nothing
to count, except those countless days and nights
that we lived through on our own, without a grain.

THE WAIT

This is the time that holds
an anxiety that speaks little
and a secret, a long-time hope.
A restlessness that would not
allow me to be myself—
all that I have been since the time
someone said, "Yours is a case of
bipolar disorder."
I always felt the necessity
of getting my daily quota
of a much-needed sleep, quietly
borrowed for a price from a drugstore
not far away from where I live.
But today everything feels
different, as if something
was going to take place,
despite the world's hopelessness
and disbelief, ironic smiles.
Something we have been waiting
for, for twenty centuries,
something that broke
the Magi's hearts over trivialities.
I know there was their faith
rather ill-placed among merely
shadowy images of despair and decay,
things they should not have believed.
As for this one who writes these
lines, there is nothing except
a faith that has lasted over
at least five decades of happiness

and pain, but more recently, pain mostly—
a pain that refuses to explain itself
but has loved to stay on with me,
as if I alone had the urgency
to wish such a wish at all.
Indeed, I wonder if it wasn't
my destiny to stay awake
through the rest of this
long, full-moon night
until I had witnessed an event
about which everyone would be
busy talking in 2050.
Sleep has already started inside
me, even as I am beginning
to be filled with prenatal secrecies.
Nonetheless I have skipped
a dinner and asked my
rather reluctant woman to keep
sitting beside me and watch
the night sky for an absent star
that is almost ready to sweep across
the eastern sky any moment now.

A DREAM OF THINGS TO COME

Who spent the long winter night
with me, all through my dream?
His transparent body shining
in the dark, his words clearly heard
by the heart? Now, I can neither recall
his features, nor remember the words.
"Can't you recall a single word?" my
wife asks. "Nothing, not a word."
But I know he was there with me
all the time, losing not a single minute
to the night. Now I feel a bit tired,
as if I hadn't had enough sleep, but
somewhere inside there is a feeling
of reassurance, a belief that
the night's dream would stay with me
notwithstanding the world's immediate
pressures, its ancient habit of
talking away everything good and fine.
It was all about me and life—a wisdom
of centuries spreading over my body
and mind in a spirit of chance and discovery.
Today, a day later, I wonder how could
the whole thing help me if I cannot
remember a thing, use what I heard
in life, could not learn a thing or two
about what I must do or should not
during the time that is still left of me.
I remember how painful the whole of
yesterday was, how far from the people
I met, how dumb and deaf, how far from
what I was going through, from every hope,

how far from what I had been until then,
how diminishing, as if there was no tomorrow!
But as I am beginning to write this line,
a voice asks me in whispers, "Do you
remember your own birth? Did you
then know how you were going to
use a new life? Must you always
struggle to know all that you are or
going to be?" And here I am and know
that I am not alone, but quite unable
to answer the questions on my own.

AT THE END OF THE WIND

A long dream of the flesh,
nerves and blood, plucked
away by a lean sharp wind
that knows its purpose
only too well to leave behind
anything except the bones
and skull, ends here, at this
precise point of stillness
and new fear, at this
early winter-morning hour.
The wind-swept pain
that seemed to pull away
the brain from its
ancestrally appointed place,
creases into a wakefulness
that locates everything
in their exact, sacred order—
as they were yesterday,
before going bed—
except this feeling of distance
from all that the mind discovers.
The hands and fingers seem
so helplessly separated from
the body they were so much
used to for so long, they
hardly know how to move
so that a line could be made,
a theme open out to the world.
A sense of being left alone
even as the houses enjoy
the last minutes of a long

and healthy night's sleep,
and a feeling of these words
being too slight and frail,
too cheerless on the page
to be noticed at all.

- A Friendship With Time -

TODAY, NOWHERE A LINE

Perhaps this is the time to sit
quietly, sipping your tea, without

waiting for anything except
a blind thought, a phrase or half-line

that amounts to little or nothing,
that may not save you from

today's absences, in utter
disregard for your need to receive

love and consolation for things
you have lost in times of crisis

in the past, indifference to even
your daily need of a beginning line,

a simple word that darkens the day
or shines in the dark of the night,

like a total solar eclipse that was
never predicted, or such a full-moon

that quietly appears only once
in eighty years, or a star

that has come too close for others'
believing, while the astrophysicists

sleep their long, intergalactic sleep.
You know that no such word is

anywhere near you for a further phrase
that you must end your

waiting with here and now. You should
feel free to look for another cup of tea.

- Bibhu Padhi -

I HEAR THE SOUND

It was a neat winter sleep
that ended a while ago.
Night is ending.
This is the time of gods
and angels celebrating
the last minutes of their
earthly sojourn.
And I hear the sound
once again, enveloping
my mind, seeping into
my body's darkest places
with a sacred touch
that would not spare
the most sinful spaces
until I felt like a feather.
A sound that is without
a source or beginning—
quiet, continuous like time.
It seems as if I am
suspended in its caring
motionlessness, enjoying
its rise and fall through
the vastness of space
and time, absorbed in its
nameless immensity.
Day is here, with its
bird-calls and vaporous
light. I know, I would be
far inside the sound's
still security until that time
when I chose to call
my night again and sleep.

- A Friendship With Time -

I know too how my dreams—
if there are any at all—
would be made of that sound
just as my sleep would be,
just as my breath is.

- Bibhu Padhi -

AFTER READING ARROGANT LINES

After you have gone through
them, it is better to stand
quiet, like the hill fronting
your house, then go on
to talk about them to their poet,
even when you are requested to,
persuaded to take each line
and image and say what you
thought of them. You should know
that there are things one cannot like,
for one never knew there could be
things beyond things, different
arousals than one is used to
over the years, feelings
that may not support the lines.
And if you did talk, beware of
all the distancing words
that would follow, the hatred
brewing inside intelligent minds
that the poems issued from
so deliberately, you could not
take them in, for you are
so different, so far from them all.
The best thing is to read the poems
and then forget them and keep your
mouth and lips closed, rest your
moving hand on your lap
or keep your two hands
as tightly interlocked as you can,
and not answer the questions at all.

LOOKING AT MYSELF

I watch myself from a distance
that is not too far for a clear sight,
nor too near so I see myself blurred.
What are the things I am made of?
Carbon. An innocent answer issues
from somewhere far from here.
I go on asking everyone what
carbon is—starting with my
twenty-year old son studying
Chemistry, and then older friends
who might know better to be able
to show me what it looks like.
And finally there are the answers.
Diamond. Graphite. Coal. Shoot.
There are other names, but they
are too hard to remember.
"Show me carbon", I say.
It is what you will be after your funeral,
polluting an air already polluted by your
desire and tendency to show off.
Ash. That is what you are and
will be, just like all that you see
here, where you have lived for
five decades and more, elsewhere—
wherever life is or supposed to be,
far from here, in the spiral galaxies,
the single stars, their solar complexities.
I look at myself in the mirror long
and hard enough to see the carbon
that I am. Everything seems simplified.

- Bibhu Padhi -

I feel my responsibility to remain
in the form so affectionately granted
by someone who loves carbon so much,
someone who so accurately weaves
so many different bodies out of what He is—
an act of pure love carried out without
effort, costing nothing, precious
like diamonds, then the feeling, I am what
He is, what, from time to time, He needs to be.

BIRTH IN OCTOBER

I never thought it could be so,
although I had been seeing
the dumb, dark-faced Brahmin
watching me over a long time, as if
he knew something I did not know.
I suppose that night was darker
than usual, noisy, the rains being
all around us, though inside
the house it was too quiet
not to feel something unusual
happening, something never
earlier heard of, written about.
Even my caring wife, waiting
beside me, did not quite know.
And then quietly, from
somewhere out of my brown body,
appeared a shape that was
so much of a daughter, it ousted
all beliefs of heretofore, all
fancies and legends, all past.
As my wife held her in her arms,
we could feel the delicate,
incandescent body, so newly ours.
Perhaps the angels had known—
flowers, like drops of soft rain,
rained over all of us; like drops of rain water,
voices from the sky poured down like greetings.
The placenta had thinned and squeezed
into a coin of shining gold. Under the light
of my daughter's impeccable body,

- Bibhu Padhi -

I gazed deep at its sides: the goddess
on one side, while the reverse held
the universe. The Brahmin walked past
the west-facing window, his eyes
asking for the infant of the night,
in exchange for the precious coin.
Our two sons held vigil all through the night.
The morning felt different; the night had
changed all. The Brahmin never came back
again, although his dark thoughts were after us.
Today, after so many nights and days,
our daughter is with us, taking care of my migraine
and melancholy, while the keen coin has been
haunting me with exotic, unshared meanings.

LIVING THROUGH THE PAIN

I do not know from where this pain
comes, but just now it is there, like love
or all that hatred means, and a bit
like greed, which likes to be everywhere.

All I know is I have to go through it
for I do not know how far I have to
travel with it. How far into the night,
how intensely, with how much blood.

I take all precautions to avoid it, but
it chooses its own minute, as if it knew
when I would least expect it, as when
I get up from bed after an afternoon sleep.

I prepare myself for every mode of escape,
every tablet, capsule, or liquid, following every
prescribed law and perceived habit, like
someone's concentrated pressure of the feet.

I do not know what I am travelling through,
or how it chose me to be a traveller through it,
except that when I was younger I boasted a lot about
how painless my life was, how much without a flaw.

Now, the prospect of further travel with it,
brings about an equivalent of fear that it might
take away my day and night, for at the same time I have
travelled through sleep too. An erratic, ill-gotten sleep.

BIRTH

I know, somewhere
last night
there was a birth.

Unnoticed, almost as if
the whole earth had fallen
into a perfectly seasonal sleep.

Someone I know
waited for it since the time
he was told that such a birth

was a painful necessity.
I know too the pain
that accompanies

every single birth. But
this one was special, like
the pain I am blessed with

but no one knows about.
What purpose does this
Christmas pain holds for me,

except that I live,
known by the world enough
to look for further celebrations?

Somewhere, an infant
as defenseless as me
is quietly growing towards

- A Friendship With Time -

a benevolence
that the world
will happen to see

for the first time
in nearly twenty centuries
of its dubious history.

- Bibhu Padhi -

AN HOUR FROM
THE END OF THE YEAR

I would rather be here,
among small words,
songs of this hour,

than sit in front of the TV
to watch "Wuthering Heights"
in the year's last night.

Some four decades ago,
it would have been
another matter.

I would have perhaps waited for
Heathcliff's return to Cathy
through a stormy night in October.

But today, I would like to be
here, among nearer things,
familiar diversions of this hour.

I know, time is everywhere—
inside yesterday, today, in
the dreams of tomorrow.

But it can merely repeat slow
meetings, quick departures,
bring back the days

from where they are—
contented, sheltered by
a talent for forgetting.

I would like to be here
rather than anywhere
near memories.

Let memories live among
their own naive homes
in a fantastic future.

- Bibhu Padhi -

STORY OF A NIGHT

My feet walked the corridor
endlessly, moving toward the room
in which she was, moving away.

The night shifted, hour by hour,
the rains increased, the nearby houses
standing like witnesses to a fear.

A long time later, I stepped inside the room,
where she sat in my bed. Blue, transparent,
her body flowing inside the room like sea-water.

I walked nearer, quietly sat beside her.
She was looking into me as if
I couldn't be anyone but herself.

Quietly I curled my arms around her,
throughout imagining the many ways
to hold an absence. Fear was so near!

And suddenly, the words, "I feel so afraid!"
I had hardly heard them before something
curled around me like a lover.

I carried her to the adjoining room where we lay
in a safer bed, each folded around the other like
leaf and bud. The night and the rains were there.

SPELLING OUT A DAY

I have been told repeatedly about
how someone who belonged
to the last century, now continues
to live with me, had practiced
the art of living, and I must confess,
living with him has been so quiet
and easy that there have been times
when I thought he was nowhere
near me. And, I can recall how
once, when we were sunbathing
one early January morning
in two cane chairs, he told me
about how precious life was,
about my inordinately long periods
of grief and loss, why I must
instruct myself to follow
a method that might bring back
the beliefs I had lost over the years.
Since that advice I have tried hard
to bring some order to my days,
stay away from my daily
thoughtlessness and inaccuracies
of habit and speech. He is still
with me, but appears pleased
with how I turn speechless before
friends I do not seem to know, things
I do not like, how I treat my
children and wife, how
neatly I spread out my days,
working on each slight moment,
as though it were infinity, how
cautiously I treat my body and myself.

- Bibhu Padhi -

A SPOT OF ANGER

It is morning here.
Summer morning and heat
and a feeling of belonging to
no one quietly haunts me.

I do not know why anger is
given to us at all, to what
purpose, if it does nothing else
but hurts. I'm afraid no one knows.

Why did it come upon me only
yesterday, when the object it could
have been directed at might have been
enjoying his comforts miles away?

I know, generations change to
turn younger, as if things that
happened to us would never happen
to them or their children, and a feeling

that the world above it is ignorant,
garrulous. I never thought so about my
father, although he died too young for me
to know him a little further, but even then

I guess he had his anger too, but I
do not remember. From whatever little
of him remains with me now, I suppose
I should have loved him a lot more.

THIS MORNING, ONCE AGAIN

It is morning and once again
I remember you. Your slow,
fond visits to your front-door
neighbors. My wife receives
you, while I am down with my
thirty-odd-years-old migraine.

Your questions and comments
are eager, intimate. "Does it happen
every day?" "I can only imagine
the pain." "What is this pain, what suffering
that may not be what one thinks it to be!"
My wife carries to me your messages of love.

This morning once again you
are not you, having taken
the straight route to heaven, its
angelic order. As far as I feel,
you have no regrets at all;
you are happy where you are.

Simple as you are, innocent as a leaf,
why should you return to this world and its
dark, devious ways, its evil eye roaming
the streets in the middle of the day, scaring
our children and us, its money-stuck ways
ignoring departures and remembrances?

Stay where you are. Keep looking
at us with your watchful, caring eye.
Send us your blessings. Let them wash

- Bibhu Padhi -

all those who miss you today, all who
loved you. Teach us how to be simple,
count our precious blessings of today.

SUNFLOWERS

It is early summer,
and the sunflowers
are waiting to turn me
into a truthful mirror.

Do the ripe flowers
know how they attract me
with the slow show
of some of their strength

from their source—
the quiet sun
and the first breeze
of spring?

I touch them
with my middle-aged
fingers. They shrink,
turn pale.

I may not touch them
again, but only stand
in front of them and
find myself imprisoned

in their flamboyant recurrence
of colours. Let them feel happy
deep inside their long season,
be left untouched by rough fingers...

- Bibhu Padhi -

SPEECH

Wherefrom this inattention
comes, so that I cannot hear
what is spoken or see
whatever is there, except
vaguely, as an afterthought?

It is neither the heart nor
the mind. The question
of the body does not arise.
It follows its routine habits,
far from the heart and the mind.

From the morning till I go to
the bed for my routine sleep.
Sometimes this sleep is not
received by the brain, having
had too much rest or meditation.

What sound is this? As if it
needed to draw me toward
a silence I have neither known
except as the one
fenced in by all other sounds.

My children and wife watch
the five kinds of sound,
at the centre of which is
the silence—undisturbed
by no one, nothing.

Outside, it is only noise,
extending beyond our world,
full of dangers and vicious
dimensions of the most unworldly kind,
connecting to no one except itself.

WITNESS

The great war has ended.
No one lost, no one won.
What do win and loss mean
to so close a picture
that held the world together?
And you, Belalsen, have seen it all—
your bodiless head watching
the pilgrimage of events
from the earth's topmost place?
You were born to be here, with
immortality in your eyes;
you are here with all of us,
with me now, and will
continue to be here
through an endless time.

Belalsen, what did you see,
what did you hear, when, on
Kurukshetra's land of truth,
the great war was on? I know
what your answer would be:
"I did not hear anything,
only saw a serrated,
razor-sharp wheel flying
from end to end, bloody with
human death, the sacrificial
animals, remaining unseen to all."

I am told you had witnessed it all
from the beginning
to the tentative end. And

the question, "What did you
see, Belalsen," was answered
so simply. "I saw nothing
except the wheel flying
to and fro, separating
the head from the body,
just as it had been in my case."

Death was everywhere
and, at the end of it all,
when some dead warriors
floated toward heaven, some
had to look into the immensities
of hell for a minute or so.
Belalsen, where are you now?

I can neither see you nor
hear you, nor do I know
what you will tell me
when my time comes to leave.
Will you witness that too?
Please do, for you shall
tell the world that here
was a man who enjoyed
everything, including
death and immortality
of the soul, who dreamt
it all, witnessed it all.

––––––––––

Based on a major character in the Indian epic, *Mahabharata.*

THE OTHER HOUR

For the first time in many years, sleep
stole itself quietly, too humbly
for an old pain. It was like a new freedom,
discovered in the hour of others' sleep,
while the rest of the night bore images
of indifference and neglect, quilt-wrapped
warmth and the true character of winter.

I think this is how one is led away
from the world's daily games, its
refusal to be other than what
it has been for years, centuries.
A mere juxtaposition of names
and dates, a cleverness that justifies
itself in the middle of every pain.

It only seems here are different tasks
for me, different guidelines to follow,
far different themes to deal with
than just heritage and poverty.
I can feel a presence that was always
there, but hazy like winter things—
a little too quiet, like death and new life.

But I hardly know why I am here, now
without my induced sleep and the dreams
that filter in invariably with a pain
that corrupts my day despite
the earthly prescriptions, until I dare to take
something that makes me forget the kidney,
the heart and liver, the brain, the body's tremour.

- Bibhu Padhi -

Even then, I have this faith somewhere still.
A faith strengthened by centuries of finding myself
for the first time, through numerous births, each
forgotten as soon as it is lived through, but joined
by the pain that heals, matures into another
for the next life. This faith in a sunlit treasure-trove
of self-perpetuating, self-annihilating mysteries.

KEEPING IN PLACE ANOTHER YEAR

Words came in this morning
in a rush as if they never
wanted to be lost to these fingers.

Words—as common as history
or lives of rocks—were there
before I was anywhere here.

Now it is early evening
and the last December sun
was lost an hour ago.

Now there is only me and those
thoughts of a year that is going to be
preserved against all odds.

A search for the right theme
competes with favourite
games, is in need of approval

from the stars and the last night
of the year. A search that knows itself
only too well for any fear of failure.

Words have dwindled into an hour
that is only on the threshold
of another day, another year.

But somewhere a voice settles into
an effortless line: "The year will remain
safe with you for several centuries."

- Bibhu Padhi -

WATCHING THE NIGHTS

Your sleepless, nightly play
worries me. Do you sleep
your long sleep in the day
because you do not like the day?

Or is it something simpler, like
the dreams you like, that
keep you warm in December?
Like giving your mother
a present of time and rest?

And do you sleep your
seven-minute sleeps
in the nights just because
your father and mother
want to enjoy a clear vacancy
of work, neglecting your play?

You need not answer, for
I am here and will know
what being with you means,
aside from watching
the night and the dark
for those angels who might
come your way, gladly stay.

A STATE OF WORSHIP

Nothing falls between the mind
and what grows on the trees
or falls to the fertile ground.
There is only this restlessness
in the midst of daily duties
of my wife, calls from children.
What is this state, this pressure
on the head that always weighs me
down to the darkness of nights?
I have asked the question to
men and men, qualified in
medicine and occult, my wife
and children: I have always
thought they know better than me.
The question rises toward heaven,
the soul's territory, the gods'
supreme privacy, their silence.
Their muteness pulls me down
to further darkness. I think
the light might be there,
the answer. Speech has vanished
like the fairytales on the mountains.
What else remains to be taken
care of, what god or goddess
needs appeasement in the
form of surrender, one that
I am so unsure of, what gift
waits to be planted on this
dry clay, devoid of blessings?

ANCIENT SOUND

This one covers me like
the luminous air, going in
through the skin

even as I breathe the January air.
It was so last year, since a time

I cannot remember.
It could be the same for all those

who watch me, ask me
to declare that all that happens,
happens to me alone.

Sure, it couldn't be so.
A voice is heard
through all that is mine—

this body, this touch,
the night air.

A voice familiar with my instincts,
guiding me as if all the days
and nights were rare.

OBSERVING A STORY

This is the small place where
all thinking stops. There are
merely amorphous impulses
that couldn't lead you anywhere.

The tissues do not follow
each other, just lie unmoved
in the skeletal dark, ready
to eat into the body.

And a little deeper down,
where a week ago happiness
stayed to greet you into
a zone of light and warmth,

winter is lisping its stories
that are nowhere centred
so they could hold the brain's
electricity, jubilant postures.

Who asks for a fibrous stillness in muscles
and nerves, the brittle thinness
of bones? Whose day brings back
only an emptiness, a folded sleep?

AN ORDINARY DAY

Stray dogs bark, the raw
announcements of candidates
for the municipal elections

pierce the afternoon air.
The new year's words
still belong to the old year.

The mind is damp
with cold and rain,
the air feels heavy.

There is no one I might
speak to, tell him my story.
There is only a wait

to have the pills as soon as
I can, feel them dissolve
inside this uninspiring body.

All the prescribed tools
are directed to an expression
of sleep and retirement.

This is the time I wait for
throughout the year—
for sleep, further sleep.

MORNING SIGNS

The night is still alive.
Darkness encloses
small roots and dreams.

Time waits, then
gives itself over
to the quietly
descending day.

Life unfolds itself again,
at all those places
where, last night, it
took over each long sleep.

The dreams spill over
to now, each fulfilled
by our wish to be
ourselves, our very own.

Is there a smell of death
somewhere, as if someone
was cooking something
with life's numerous ways?

Is there someone yet
who hasn't slept at all through
the night's games—
somewhat like myself?

- Bibhu Padhi -

ECHOES OF HAPPINESS

The sky is filled with
bird wings, while
the songs fall on the valley.

There are promises
to be taken care of, arranged
in their exulting order.

At the end of the day,
the songs enclose
the town, the hills.

There is peace here,
regardless of the sorrows
elsewhere.

We listen to the songs
even as echoes of happiness
fall on our heart and skin.

The skin glows just as
the day does, their touch
as remote as the hills.

WATCHING WATER IN SUMMER

You will have to leave
everything, including
your ambitions for the day,
and watch its fall in a thin line
from the brass tap,
collecting in, filling,
the small red buckets. Slow,
like the hour hand on your
Titan watch,
as if it didn't move at all,
as if the loss of water
was too trivial
to be recorded by its time.
And then, suddenly, outside,
this miracle of space,
the sky bursting with
this thundershower--
far from all deserts,
even thoughts of deserts,
and of those places where
men, women and children
walk their long miles
to places where water
emerges, like weak leaves,
as their waiting lingers,
where the seed has forgotten
its own source, its former life
within the dark, moist earth,
the ancient river.
Quietly, purposelessly,
you return to the water

gathering in your
own plastic buckets in drops,
in thin lines, and, as you watch
their fall, you recall
from time to time, your
old thirst, feeling how precious
watching the water
falling can be--
just a thin line of simple water
falling on the dark skin of the floor.

A FRIENDSHIP WITH TIME

From a place within this night
that I have not known previously,
a casual question arrives: "Would you
know me?" The voice seems gentle,
motionless, familiar, as true and right
as the stars and the galaxies, as near as air.
It is difficult to place it among
the remembered noises of the world,
its selfish motives, harsh absences.
Could it be someone's whom I might have
Forgotten, taken for granted, just as
so many others have taken me
since a time I can remember?
A feeling of guilt rises from somewhere
inside this mind, this heart.
The question haunts my innocence
and privacy, keeps repeating itself from
all that is with me, all around me.
From the sleep of my children and wife,
their simple breathings, the stacks of books
I have piled over the years in order to
make myself wise, the walls and the ceilings,
memories of lost trees, the bed in which
I have learnt to lie without sleep, my mouth
and lips: "Would you know me?" It is
much closer now, as if it were next to me,
like a friend or lover whom I had lost
in my effort to prove myself to the world,
among conquests and defeats, pleasure
and hurt, the pain of forgetting, my
inability to move within, stay happy

with myself, my countless stupidities.
How do I answer the question? Words
are too far from me now than they were
an hour ago. "You do not need words for
love and friendship." A reassurance that
I have never had so affectionately, embraces
every limb and eye, ever so gently touching
my toes and fingertips, breathing through my
heart, mind and body. Breath meets breath.
I recollect. Words are few. But then, a pair of
remote lips, shy like the night, somehow whispers,
"Yes, oh yes, dear friend, I know you."